52 VERSES ON HOPE

fifty two devotionals
that will inspire hope

SAMUEL DEUTH

ISBN 978-1-64744-127-2

Published by Outreach, Inc. Colorado Springs, CO 80919
www.Outreach.com

Interior Design by Alexia Garaventa

BEFORE YOU BEGIN

These fifty-two Bible verses take you on a journey of HOPE throughout the Bible! They will encourage and call you to put your hope in Christ alone.

You can go through the book daily and then read through it multiple times in a year, or you can read each verse for a week and memorize it before you move on to the next verse.

As you read the verse and devotional, be sure to take the time to ask and answer the questions. The power of God's Word is in the application of its truths. If you are not familiar with a mentioned person or story, use the verse reference to look up the story in your Bible or ask a pastor, Bible study leader, or another believer about the story.

Included with each verse is a confession of faith section. These are truths based on that verse that will shape and guide your life!

1

**"Hope in the Lord and keep his way.
He will exalt you to inherit the land;
when the wicked are destroyed,
you will see it."**

Psalm 37:34

DEVOTION

Great hope is found on God's path. When we follow the Bible, we'll find that we can be safe and secure in what we do. You may want to be hopeful, but if we don't follow His path, we'll find ourselves slipping. You may even wonder why God is doing this to you; it's because while we said we trust God, we didn't obey His Word. If you put your hope in God and follow His ways, you'll inherit the land (Psalm 37:9)! The way of the wicked will always end in death, but you can trust that God's path always leads to victory.

QUESTIONS

Have you started reading the Bible? Consider starting a Bible reading plan. The Bible gives us the best path for life. What new habits from the Bible are you wanting to apply to your life?

CONFESSION

I will carefully live according to God's ways. He will elevate and establish my life.

2

"Why, my soul, are you downcast? Why so disturbed within me? Put your hope in God, for I will yet praise him, my Savior and my God."

Psalm 42:5

DEVOTION

King David ruled over ancient Israel and was known as a great writer of prayers and songs throughout his life. In this verse, King David articulates the battle of being led by our emotions rather than by God's character. He asks a great question of himself: "Why are you so depressed?" Rather than just being led by his internal emotions, he challenges and questions them and calls himself back to the truth. Rather than losing hope, he stirs it back up and tells it where to rest. He's challenging himself to put his hope back in God rather than the circumstances or the person that had hurt or wronged him. It takes intentionality to retrain your mind!

QUESTIONS

Take time to evaluate the state of your soul. Are you feeling full of joy or overwhelmed? How are you keeping your soul and body refreshed?

CONFESSION

I will not be led by my emotions; I will put my hope in God.

3

"The wicked go down to the realm of the dead, all the nations that forget God. But God will never forget the needy; the hope of the afflicted will never perish. Arise, Lord, do not let mortals triumph; let the nations be judged in your presence."

Psalm 9:17-19

DEVOTION

God is the hope of the afflicted! God isn't just interested in you when you win and are on top of the world. Sometimes in life, we can find ourselves being so performance-driven that we wonder if God is just the hope of the heroes and the happy, but He is also your hope when you feel like you've reached the end of your rope. God does not shy away from our mess and challenges, but He is available to heal you and respond to your cry for help.

QUESTIONS

When have you experienced a loss or failure? Share how you felt and how God comforted you. How have you learned to heal and regain your hope?

CONFESSION

Even if I fail, God will protect me and never forget me.

4

"No king is saved by the size of his army; no warrior escapes by his great strength. A horse is a vain hope for deliverance; despite all its great strength it cannot save. But the eyes of the Lord are on those who fear him, on those whose hope is in his unfailing love."

Psalm 33:16-18

DEVOTION

What are you putting your hope in? What are you resting your confidence and trust in? Is it in the modern-day version of the horse, which would be our careers, education, or family ties? On this side of eternity, while we need protection and security, ultimately our salvation comes from God. So many times in Israel's history, they were outmanned and overpowered, but God gave them victory. Keep building and expanding your skills and abilities, but put your hope in God.

QUESTIONS

Have you ever felt overpowered? Have you ever put your trust in the wrong person or skill or job? What happened?

CONFESSION

My trust is not in the strength of my hand but in the power of my God!

5

"To deliver them from death and keep them alive in famine. We wait in hope for the Lord; he is our help and our shield. In him our hearts rejoice, for we trust in his holy name."

Psalm 33:19-21

DEVOTION

You can put your hope in God no matter the season you find yourself in. Even in a famine, God is able. If we're not careful, we'll say we trust God, and then when we see a news story or the stock market update, we go to fear. It's as if we're assuming that God can help us only when the economy is good. But God is Lord over all of the elements and nations. Keep fighting to put your hope in God in the good seasons and the difficult seasons. Whether the doctor's report or the financial report is good or bad, return to God and put your trust in Him.

QUESTIONS

What's the most difficult time you've found yourself in? How did God help you through it? What difficulty do you need God to redeem or heal right now?

CONFESSION

I wait in great expectation for God's deliverance!

6

"'She is in bitter distress, but the LORD has hidden it from me and has not told me why.' 'Did I ask you for a son, my lord?' she said. 'Didn't I tell you, "Don't raise my hopes"?'"

2 Kings 4:27-28

DEVOTION

"Don't get your hopes up" is a phrase that we often hear in our culture. It's an attempt to stop our risk of disappointment and pain. But this phrase is a trick of the enemy to rob your life. God calls us to great faith, and the devil is always going to tempt you to play it small and safe. Hope is the building block that purpose and potential are built on, so the devil is going to try to steal your hope. Even when you're facing what might seem like the death of your dream, don't lose hope! Remember, God is faithful.

QUESTIONS

What dream or promise has God given you? Have you walked through a season where your dream was lost? Share about it.

CONFESSION

I will keep my hopes up because my hope is in God!

7

"Why do I put myself in jeopardy and take my life in my hands? Though he slay me, yet will I hope in him; I will surely defend my ways to his face. Indeed, this will turn out for my deliverance, for no godless person would dare come before him!"

Job 13:14-16

DEVOTION

Job is a man in the Bible who was very prosperous but experienced severe trials and lost everything, including his family. The journey Job walks through is almost unimaginable! Yet through it all, he maintains an unshakable view of God's ultimate goodness. Even though Job is seeing a steady stream of evil coming his way, he anchors his hope in God's track record of goodness toward the godly. This verse is also a testament to Job's surrender to God's wisdom and insight being beyond his own. Why would Job say, "Even if He kills me, I'll hope in Him"? Because he's saying, "I may not understand it all, but I will trust Him."

QUESTIONS

When is a time that God has been good and blessed your life? Is there any area of your life that you still need to surrender to God?

CONFESSION

I will put my hope in God even when I don't understand everything He's doing.

8

"For what you have done I will always praise you in the presence of your faithful people. And I will hope in your name, for your name is good."

Psalm 52:9

DEVOTION

God is good! This is a truth we know by how God has revealed Himself to us in the Bible and throughout human history. But, it's also the key thing that the devil is always trying to challenge. With Adam and Eve, the devil tried to say that God was holding out on them. And he continues to repeat that lie. However, not only is God good, but He is working out good for you and has been working toward good from the beginning of time. Take time to reflect on the good that He's done in your life and those around you, and watch how hope begins to rise in your heart again!

QUESTIONS

What are three things you are thankful for? And what are three things you are worried about that you could turn over to God? Write them down.

CONFESSION

You are a good God! All you say and do can be trusted.

9

"Yes, my soul, find rest in God;
my hope comes from him."

Psalm 62:5

DEVOTION

From time to time you may feel like you don't even have the ability to hope anymore. But that's how good God is—not only is He the one that we want to put our hope in, but He is also the giver of hope. When you're up against a wall and feeling overwhelmed, lean into and spend time with Jesus. He will pour hope into your heart once again! Notice how King David, the author of this psalm, commands his soul: you don't have to be run by your emotions; tell your soul where to go for hope!

QUESTIONS

Are you taking time to rest? If not, make it a priority to carve out some time for resting and spending time in prayer and reading the Bible. How can you become more consistent in church attendance, Bible reading, and prayer?

CONFESSION

God is where my soul truly finds rest and refreshing. My hope comes from God.

10

"You answer us with awesome and righteous deeds, God our Savior, the hope of all the ends of the earth and of the farthest seas."

Psalm 65:5

DEVOTION

This verse reminds us that He is an answering God. He's not distant and silent and uninterested; He's present and answering in abundant fashion. Also, notice that God is not just our hope in whatever nation you're reading this, but God is the hope of all people in all nations. It is the heart and desire of heaven to have all nations in relationship with God and for everyone to experience His hope.

QUESTIONS

What is a recent prayer God answered that you can stop and be thankful for? What's one situation that you need wisdom, healing, or help from God?

CONFESSION

God loves to hear from me and will answer my prayer. You are the hope of the nations!

11

"For you have been my hope, Sovereign Lord, my confidence since my youth."

Psalm 71:5

DEVOTION

You may not have known God since your youth, but you can be confident that no matter when you connected with God, He will be faithful through every age—just like a parent to a child. Each season of our development is going to need something different from a parent, and God is ready to meet each need in your life through all of the seasons. Also note that if God has been faithful to King David since his youth, that means God is gracious with our immaturities and issues and will walk through it all, upholding His goodness even when we fail.

QUESTIONS

Was there a time as a child that you felt alone? Talk about that. When has God felt close to you?

CONFESSION

God is personally walking with me in all seasons of life! I will put my hope in His faithfulness!

12

"May my accusers perish in shame; may those who want to harm me be covered with scorn and disgrace. As for me, I will always have hope; I will praise you more and more. My mouth will tell of your righteous deeds, of your saving acts all day long—though I know not how to relate them all."

Psalm 71:13-15

DEVOTION

Why is King David, the writer of this psalm, declaring hope? Because he understands the nature of God. While God judges and condemns the wicked, David also knows that God blesses and strengthens the righteous. His hope is in God and His ability and desire to bless and strengthen you. Even when evil is coming against you, don't fear because God is working toward your good. I love that in this verse, David declares, "I will always have hope." He's saying, "No matter what the future holds, I am secure because I know who holds the future!"

QUESTIONS

Did you grow up believing that God wanted to bless you? Do you see God as tolerating you or as available to save and rescue you?

CONFESSION

I will always have hope because God is always with me!

13

“Know also that wisdom is like honey for you: If you find it, there is a future hope for you, and your hope will not be cut off.”

Proverbs 24:14

DEVOTION

We see here that hope is a by-product of wisdom. Hope is not a feeling that's disconnected from reality; it's a feeling and expectation that flows from a life of wisdom. When I know that I'm living right and according to God's Word, it gives me hope and confidence that the outcome of what I'm going after will be successful. The more wisdom and counsel that you embrace, the greater the hope of victory is and the greater the faith you can take on the future with. You don't have to live in dread of what will or could happen, but you can have great hope because you are walking in wisdom.

QUESTIONS

Have you asked God for wisdom? What is He saying? Who can you set an appointment with to seek counsel from?

CONFESSION

God, I will seek your wisdom and find hope!

14

“My soul faints with longing for your salvation, but I have put my hope in your word.”

Psalm 119:81

DEVOTION

Sometimes we're afraid to be honest about where we're at in life. But King David shows us how to be vulnerable with the heaviness or pain that we're walking through. He then directs himself back to hope in God. And right now, no matter what you may be facing, you may feel like David, where you're about to faint—but don't let your feelings tell you where to hope; put your hope in God today!

QUESTIONS

When was a time you almost quit, but you made it through? Do you have a favorite inspirational quote or expression? Identify two or three Bible verses you can learn and repeat often to build your faith.

CONFESSION

Even when I feel tired, God will remain faithful.

15

“I rise before dawn and cry for help;
I have put my hope in your word.”

Psalm 119:147

DEVOTION

Is your daily routine intentional? King David gives us a window into how he keeps a life full of hope. Instead of waking up aimlessly or waking up and focusing on the negative, he wakes up and cries out to God right away! If you create a rhythm of getting in your daily Bible reading and prayer as the first thing, you'll set up your day to thrive. There are principles of first and focus. What you put your focus on first will set the flow for the rest of your day.

QUESTIONS

What's one thing you need to add to your daily routine? What's one thing you need to remove from your daily habits?

CONFESSION

I will daily call out to the Lord and put my hope in Him!

16

"Israel, put your hope in the LORD, for with the LORD is unfailing love and with him is full redemption."

Psalm 130:7

DEVOTION

Are you calling others to hope? There's a lot packed into this verse, but let's focus on the fact that King David is directing and challenging his nation to put their hope in God. We're often made to believe that we just need to pause and focus on ourselves and then help others later once we're good. But, throughout the Bible, we see that God uses us even as we're walking through difficulty. We get strengthened as we serve others. God called and activated Gideon before he felt strong (Judges 6). The Apostle Paul said God's strength is made perfect in my weakness (2 Corinthians 12:9).

QUESTIONS

Who can you encourage to put their hope in God today? Who can you add value to?

CONFESSION

I will call people to put their hope in the unfailing love of God!

17

"The Lord delights in those who fear him, who put their hope in his unfailing love."

Psalm 147:11

DEVOTION

When you decide to honor and fear the Lord, it sets the rest of your life in order. The book of Proverbs teaches us that trusting the Lord is the beginning of wisdom (Proverbs 9:10). The words *hope* and *trust* are strongly linked. When I put my trust and hope in the Lord, I will live with a greater sense of peace and mercy in my life. The end of this verse is where all the confidence lies: "his unfailing love." God's love is eternal, never-ending, and unfailing. Even if I fail, He won't.

QUESTIONS

Do you find it difficult to trust the Bible? Why or why not? Is there a section of the Bible that you're currently having a difficult time with?

CONFESSION

I will submit my life fully to God! His ways are higher and more reliable than mine. My hope is in His love.

18

"Hopes placed in mortals die with them; all the promise of their power comes to nothing."

Proverbs 11:7

DEVOTION

Where is your hope placed today? Is it in the temporary or the eternal? Often to get the right view of something, we have to elevate our perspective. We need to see it from above. When you're down in the weeds of life, it's easy to get overwhelmed and to lose sight of where you're going. This is why we put our hope in God rather than humans. It's only in God, who has the elevated and eternal view, that we can be assured and confident of the wisdom and insight that we're getting. Trust in God's Word.

QUESTIONS

Was there a time when you determined to trust God's Word over your own? Explain. What wisdom do you need from God right now?

CONFESSION

God, you are sure and reliable! When I trust you, I won't be disappointed.

19

**“Hope deferred makes the heart sick,
but a longing fulfilled is a tree of life.”**

Proverbs 13:12

DEVOTION

Many are disheartened and discouraged because of unfulfilled hopes and dreams. But we see clearly that God loves to see your desires fulfilled. You're not fighting against God to do and accomplish what's in your heart; you're working with Him. If you're currently experiencing delays in your dream, get some outside counsel or coaching to help you determine if you need to maintain course and stay faithful or if you need to change and adjust how you're thinking or acting to see your hopes fulfilled.

QUESTIONS

Have you wished or hoped for something that didn't come true? Share about it. Now, what is a goal that you're going to go after with renewed hope?

CONFESSION

I will thank God for hopes fulfilled, and I will trust God when dreams are delayed.

20

“Never take your word of truth from my mouth, for I have put my hope in your laws.”

Psalm 119:43

DEVOTION

King David knew how essential God's Word is. So much so that he says, "Never take your word from my mouth." The way he describes his hope in God's Word is powerful. He knows where to put his hope. Often we're caught in trouble because we're putting our hope and trust in all the wrong things. It's a good reminder that if you're feeling tired or weary, it could be an indicator that you've placed your trust in the natural rather than the supernatural power and principles of God.

QUESTIONS

How often are you engaging with the Bible? What's one of your favorite verses and why?

CONFESSION

God's Word is powerful and gives me hope! I will daily speak the truth from the Bible.

21

“Anyone who is among the living has hope—even a live dog is better off than a dead lion!”

Ecclesiastes 9:4

DEVOTION

If you're still breathing, you have reason to hope. We love the strength of lions and the majesty that they carry. We can often look at our own lives and feel a lack of hope or strength because we're not the lion or because we see ourselves more like the dog in comparison. But if you're alive, you have a chance for victory. Don't worry if you're the lion or the dog; just be concerned with if you're breathing. God can do anything He wants with your life. He used a small teenager to defeat a giant warrior and to save a nation (1 Samuel 17). Don't doubt what God can do in and through your life!

QUESTIONS

Have you allowed comparison to rob you of your purpose? Who inspires you?

CONFESSION

I will honor God with every breath that I have. As long as I am living, I have purpose and potential!

22

"Do you not know? Have you not heard? The Lord is the everlasting God, the Creator of the ends of the earth. He will not grow tired or weary, and his understanding no one can fathom. He gives strength to the weary and increases the power of the weak. Even youths grow tired and weary, and young men stumble and fall; but those who hope in the Lord will renew their strength. They will soar on wings like eagles; they will run and not grow weary, they will walk and not be faint."

Isaiah 40:28-31

DEVOTION

The Bible says that the joy of the Lord is our strength (Nehemiah 8:10). Hope is in the same vein as joy. When our hope disappears, we'll find ourselves tired and losing the strength, both physically and mentally, to take on the adventures and challenges of life. The encouraging thing about this verse is that if your hope has weakened, it can be strengthened again. It is renewable. And God is the source of the supply of that hope. Look to Jesus and your hope will return, and with that hope, strength will be renewed in you!

QUESTIONS

What do you do to get refreshed physically and mentally? Are there songs you like to play to put yourself in a good mood? Make plans today for the next time you'll spend time with God to renew your spirit.

CONFESSION

I may get weary, but my strength will be renewed as I put my hope in God!

23

"Do any of the worthless idols of the nations bring rain? Do the skies themselves send down showers? No, it is you, LORD our God. Therefore our hope is in you, for you are the one who does all this."

Jeremiah 14:22

DEVOTION

God is our source of life and provision. Take inventory of the things you've been putting your confidence in—is it giving you good results? Look to the fruit and results of God's Word and promises. Jesus encouraged us to judge a tree by its fruit. Jesus said that He is the vine and we are the branches (John 15:5). This means that we must stay connected to Him to be fresh, alive, and producing results. If you're finding your life, relationships, work, and health are suffering, take the time to make sure you're connected to the vine, which is Jesus.

QUESTIONS

What miracles have you seen God do in your life or in the lives of those around you? What provision do you need right now that you can begin to pray about?

CONFESSION

My hope is in God, the source of blessing and provision!

24

“‘For I know the plans I have for you,’ declares the LORD, ‘plans to prosper you and not to harm you, plans to give you hope and a future.’”

Jeremiah 29:11

DEVOTION

God's plan is for your good! Don't buy into the lie that God wants you to suffer or be in lack. He may take you through a valley or a storm, but He's always leading you toward peace and the blessing of God. This verse is a promise that we must learn to hold onto with all that we have. Even if the current circumstance isn't good, when God is working through the duration of your life, He's always leading toward green pastures—for your good and His glory.

QUESTIONS

Did you grow up thinking that God wanted good for your life? Or how did you see Him? Is there a good desire in your heart that you need to chase again?

CONFESSION

God has intentional plans to bring good into my life!

"I well remember them, and my soul is downcast within me. Yet this I call to mind and therefore I have hope: Because of the LORD's great love we are not consumed, for his compassions never fail."

Lamentations 3:20-22

DEVOTION

If we're going to be overflowing with hope, we have to learn how to call to mind the right things. We are constantly bombarded with the wrong thoughts and negative messaging that drain our strength. So, learn to identify when the wrong thoughts are coming your way, and direct your mind and heart toward what is good. One of the key things to keep focused on that will bring hope is the love of God. It's because of His love that we are not consumed. His love and grace hold us together.

QUESTIONS

Would you rather spend time with positive- or negative-minded people? Do you find it easier to focus on the good or the negative in your life? Write out the confession and repeat it daily for a week.

CONFESSION

The love of God is great and never-ending! I will put my hope in His faithfulness.

26

"So I prophesied as he commanded me, and breath entered them; they came to life and stood up on their feet—a vast army. Then he said to me: 'Son of man, these bones are the people of Israel. They say, "Our bones are dried up and our hope is gone; we are cut off." Therefore prophesy and say to them: "This is what the Sovereign LORD says: My people, I am going to open your graves and bring you up from them; I will bring you back to the land of Israel."'"

Ezekiel 37:10-12

DEVOTION

We must learn to declare and prophesy the Word of God over our lives rather than echoing the words of our culture. In this valley, the dry bones were the reality. Sometimes we come face-to-face with the deadness of our circumstances, feeling like all hope is lost. But we must go to God and His Word, find His promises for our lives, and hold onto them. Things may look dry, but if you have a promise from God, begin to speak that out and declare it. God's Word can bring hopeless things back to life! This is the power of God's Word in your mouth!

QUESTIONS

What is something the world tells you is true that contradicts God's Word? What is something you think is dead in your life? Find a verse that breathes life over your circumstances.

CONFESSION

God can bring dry and dead things back to life. I will prophesy God's Word over my life!

27

"A bruised reed he will not break, and a smoldering wick he will not snuff out, till he has brought justice through to victory. In his name the nations will put their hope."

Matthew 12:20-22

DEVOTION

Jesus is the hope of all people in all nations. He is and always will be the true and only solution to the brokenness of mankind. But Jesus' sacrifice is sufficient for everyone. The enemy thought that he would be able to break and end the prophetic fulfillment of the Messiah, but in crucifying Jesus, the full strength of the power of the blood of Jesus was released to heal and save. Today, put your hope in the name of Jesus!

QUESTIONS

What are the biggest challenges facing your city? How can you do your part to bring Jesus and biblical principles into your city?

CONFESSION

I will put my hope in the God of justice and mercy!

28

"David said about him: 'I saw the Lord always before me. Because he is at my right hand, I will not be shaken. Therefore my heart is glad and my tongue rejoices; my body also will rest in hope, because you will not abandon me to the realm of the dead, you will not let your holy one see decay.'"

Acts 2:25-27

DEVOTION

We often underestimate the toll that life can have on us. Work, family, the economy, school, and the news can all begin to drain our energy. When we put our hope in Jesus, it affects our heart and emotions; it changes how we speak; and it impacts the physical body's ability to rest. When we learn to set our minds on the faithfulness of God, it will allow us to enter into greater levels of rest. The Bible says that He grants sleep to those He loves (Psalm 127:2). You don't need to run the planet or solve all the problems; allow God to run the universe, and choose to entrust your life into His hands.

QUESTIONS

Do you have a good rhythm of rest? What's something God has spoken to you during your devotional time?

CONFESSION

I am unshakable because my hope is in the unshakable God!

29

"Against all hope, Abraham in hope believed and so became the father of many nations, just as it had been said to him, 'So shall your offspring be.'"

Romans 4:18

DEVOTION

What a powerful verse! Against all odds, Abraham goes all in! Abraham was over eighty and had no children, but God promised to make a huge nation from his descendants and Abraham believed God! So now we know him as the father of the faith. That title came because he chose to stare fear in the face and keep trusting God. Much of your calling and breakthrough is on the other side of what seems hopeless. But the only situation that is truly hopeless is when God isn't involved. When the doctor says there's nothing they can do or the bank says there's no way, that's when you lean in even harder to the promises of God and keep believing!

QUESTIONS

What is the most daring thing or mission you've ever attempted? When did you trust God and go for it even when it seemed impossible?

CONFESSION

No matter what circumstances look like in the natural, I will put my hope in the promise-keeping God!

30

"Not only so, but we also glory in our sufferings, because we know that suffering produces perseverance; perseverance, character; and character, hope. And hope does not put us to shame, because God's love has been poured out into our hearts through the Holy Spirit, who has been given to us."

Romans 5:3-5

DEVOTION

When you trust God, hope is an end product of life's trials. Instead of these circumstances taking us out, they begin to produce perseverance and character that shape our hope. It says hope doesn't disappoint. What does that mean? The kind of hope that is shaped over trials and time isn't a weak hope. It's a sure and solid hope that is built on the track record of God. This kind of hope will not disappoint when you're facing trials. Stay in the game, don't give up, and watch God faithfully fulfill His promises to you.

QUESTIONS

Are you a persistant person who doesn't give up, or are you more easy going? What's an area of your character that God has been developing? Ask the Holy Spirit to fill you with hope and His love!

CONFESSION

Patience produces godly character and a sure hope!

31

"For in this hope we were saved. But hope that is seen is no hope at all. Who hopes for what they already have?"

Romans 8:24

DEVOTION

We're being challenged here—in a good way! The Apostle Paul, who wrote this verse, is saying that if your hope is in just what you can see in the natural world, that's not true hope and faith. Hope is a trust in the God of the universe's ability to keep His Word. Jesus often commended those who trusted before seeing or even without seeing. God can truly work through the individual willing to take Him at His Word. If God promised it to you in the Bible and by His Spirit but you're not seeing it yet, keep trusting and hoping in Jesus.

QUESTIONS

What is your favorite Bible promise? What is a promise from God that you don't see yet but that you're still believing for? Ask your friends their passion and pray and fight with them!

CONFESSION

My hope isn't built on circumstances but on God's faithfulness.

32

“Be joyful in hope, patient in affliction, faithful in prayer.”

Romans 12:12

DEVOTION

Worship while you wait! While you're waiting for that thing you're hoping for, keep praising. All through Scripture God highlights worship and thankfulness. When Jesus heals ten lepers and only one comes back to say thank you, Jesus asks where the rest of them are (Luke 17:17). For the thankful one, Jesus both heals and brings salvation. King David calls us to enter into God's presence with thanksgiving and praise (Psalm 95:2). Are we going to complain while we wait, or are we going to be joyful in hope?

QUESTIONS

When's the last time you thanked God without being prompted? What is an over-the-top offering you could bring God to thank and praise Him?

CONFESSION

I will be thankful and worship while I wait for the promises of God to be fulfilled.

33

"For everything that was written in the past was written to teach us, so that through the endurance taught in the Scriptures and the encouragement they provide we might have hope."

Romans 15:4

DEVOTION

Take trips back in time to remember the faithfulness of God in your life and the lives of others. The Bible was written to give you hope. When I revisit the stories of God's power, faithfulness, grace, and provision, it calls me toward hope. The Bible teaches us that faith comes by hearing (Romans 10:17), and so does hope. Hope stirs up and increases faith in my heart the more I remember how He has carried the men and women of faith in the Bible and throughout modern history. Become a student of God's goodness to others, and it will give you hope to believe for it to be repeated in your life!

QUESTIONS

Take time to read the first four books of the New Testament, also known as the Gospels, to be reminded of Jesus' desire to forgive, heal, and set you free! What's one thing you've learned in the waiting?

CONFESSION

My hope increases when I endure and stay faithful!

34

"May the God of hope fill you with all joy and peace as you trust in him, so that you may overflow with hope by the power of the Holy Spirit."

Romans 15:13

DEVOTION

A life of hope in God produces joy and peace. The Holy Spirit causes us to overflow with hope. In modern self-help teaching, it's purely up to you to make all of the happiness and hope happen. But we see that hope is more of a flow from the Holy Spirit that produces that life of joy and peace than it is about you trying to be happy in yourself. Have you invited the Holy Spirit to come and fill you and empower you? Learning to surrender to the Holy Spirit is central to this life of hope! Hope is from Him.

QUESTIONS

How have you learned to trust God more in your daily decisions? What areas of trust are you still working on? Spend some time this week praying in the Spirit and just being in His presence.

CONFESSION

He is the God of hope. I will walk in joy and peace as I trust Him!

35

"Surely he says this for us, doesn't he? Yes, this was written for us, because whoever plows and threshes should be able to do so in the hope of sharing in the harvest."

1 Corinthians 9:10

DEVOTION

The principle of seedtime and harvest has been established by God. He teaches us to expect a harvest from our seed. And in your life, He wants you to live with an expectant hope of the fruits of your labors. You don't have to do what's right without any hope that good will come of it. When dreams and harvest get delayed, we get discouraged and that is a killer of hope. God has designed and determined that you have a hope of reward for your investment.

QUESTIONS

What are you expecting God to do in this season? What are you hoping to see happen in your life, work, and areas of service in the next few months?

CONFESSION

I will share the rewards of my work. I will reap what I sow.

36

"Love is patient, love is kind. It does not envy, it does not boast, it is not proud. It does not dishonor others, it is not self-seeking, it is not easily angered, it keeps no record of wrongs. Love does not delight in evil but rejoices with the truth. It always protects, always trusts, always hopes, always perseveres. Love never fails. But where there are prophecies, they will cease; where there are tongues, they will be stilled; where there is knowledge, it will pass away."

1 Corinthians 13:1-8

DEVOTION

Our relationships thrive on love and hope. True love always hopes for the best and wants the best for you. When the people in your life can sense that you are believing the best about them and hoping for good for them, it's an empowering and freeing thing. Have you lost hope for a friend? Have you lost hope for your marriage? If you feel something getting dry or difficult, add some faith into it and watch it come alive. Just like a plant that is wilting because it's low on water, a relationship without hope will begin to wilt.

QUESTIONS

Read over the verse multiple times this week. What is God highlighting to you? In what ways could you show more love and hope in your relationships?

CONFESSION

I will choose to hope and believe the best about the people in my life. I will speak life over them!

37

“If only for this life we have hope in Christ, we are of all people most to be pitied.”

1 Corinthians 15:19

DEVOTION

Your hope is not temporary. Your hope in Jesus is not just a feel-good fairy tale that numbs the pain of earth. Your hope is eternal. The Apostle Paul says if we're just doing religion for this life, people should feel sorry for us. But our hope is for life and the life to come. Jesus came for both here and now and then and there. And while we're here, Jesus tells us to pray for His kingdom to come on earth (Matthew 6:10)! Christianity is to impact every part of your life. It's for the physical and the natural day-to-day that we all face. God has answers for every day.

QUESTIONS

Reflect on a job, person, or circumstance that you thought was forever but ended up being temporary. How did you feel when it ended? What are you most looking forward to in heaven?

CONFESSION

My hope is Jesus so my hope is eternal!

38

"Therefore, since we have such a hope, we are very bold."

2 Corinthians 3:12

DEVOTION

My hope in Jesus gives me courage! Because I know who's behind me, I'm full of hope. It reminds me of the story of David and Goliath; although he was young and much smaller, David had confidence that he could beat the giant Goliath because God was on David's side. In your life, you'll know that you're starting to live and walk in greater hope when you begin to live with less fear and more courage. Courage in what you say and in what you do should be a by-product of knowing God more. The Old Testament prophet Daniel, who faced his fears in the lions' den, said that the people who know their God will be mighty (Daniel 11:32)!

QUESTIONS

What's the difference between arrogance and boldness? What past victory has God given you that gives you boldness to take on the future?

CONFESSION

I will put my hope in God and walk in boldness!

39

"For through the Spirit we eagerly await by faith the righteousness for which we hope."

Galatians 5:5

DEVOTION

The Holy Spirit continues to be a theme connected to the topic of hope. Through Him, we are encouraged and given the ability to wait for the hope to be fulfilled. The more we lean into the voice of the Holy Spirit, the more at peace we will be in our day-to-day lives. The Bible calls us to keep in step with the Spirit (Galatians 5:25). When He steps, you step. He will guide and direct you onto the right path. It's the Holy Spirit that walks with us on earth toward our ultimate salvation and heaven.

QUESTIONS

Is prayer a first response when you experience trouble? How do you know when the Holy Spirit is speaking to you? Ask the Holy Spirit to fill the room where you're at right now and give you peace and rest.

CONFESSION

The Holy Spirit is perfecting me. I walk in the righteousness that Jesus gave me.

40

"I keep asking that the God of our Lord Jesus Christ, the glorious Father, may give you the Spirit of wisdom and revelation, so that you may know him better. I pray that the eyes of your heart may be enlightened in order that you may know the hope to which he has called you, the riches of his glorious inheritance in his holy people, and his incomparably great power for us who believe."

Ephesians 1:17-19

DEVOTION

What a great hope we have been called to! Often we forget to reflect on His goodness. Our hope in Jesus is of eternal significance! Because of our sin, we had been condemned to hell and eternal separation from God. We were lost and without hope. But, because of Jesus, we have overcome this unpayable debt. Jesus came as the perfect Lamb of God to become the eternal and once-for-all sacrifice for the sin of humanity. If we put our hope in Him, we'll be saved, healed, forgiven, and set completely free from the grip that Satan had on us.

QUESTIONS

Have you given your life to Jesus? What are you most thankful for about your relationship with God?

CONFESSION

I will walk in the fullness of all that Jesus paid for on the cross.

"Remember that at that time you were separate from Christ, excluded from citizenship in Israel and foreigners to the covenants of the promise, without hope and without God in the world."

Ephesians 2:12

DEVOTION

The purest form of hopelessness isn't that things are difficult but that Jesus is not present. No matter the circumstance, if God is with you, you don't need to feel hopeless. If you've found Christ, then you've found pure hope. Look around you today and ask God to give you eyes to see others in your family, work, or community who are away from Jesus and without hope. How can you reach out today and invite them to come to church with you? Our world is dealing with all kinds of depression and anxiety from a lack of hope. And Jesus is the true answer to the pain and longing of their hearts.

QUESTIONS

Who in your world needs Jesus? What was the moment that led you to Christ?

CONFESSION

I have great hope! Jesus paid the debt of my sin.

42

"If you continue in your faith, established and firm, and do not move from the hope held out in the gospel. This is the gospel that you heard and that has been proclaimed to every creature under heaven, and of which I, Paul, have become a servant."

Colossians 1:23

DEVOTION

We live in an instant world. We enjoy most things right away with little wait. But most of the calling and purpose that God has for you is going to be birthed over time. And in that process of time is where your character development happens. It's also where we can tend to get weary and lose hope. But, in all of the seasons and trials of life, keep holding onto the hope that Jesus holds out to us—which is that He loves us so much that He came to be with us and bring us close to Him! He's holding out the hope, but are you receiving it?

QUESTIONS

Are you frustrated with delays or patient with the process? What's something that was worth the wait?

CONFESSION

I will continue in faith. I will put my hope in the good news of Jesus!

43

“We remember before our God and Father your work produced by faith, your labor prompted by love, and your endurance inspired by hope in our Lord Jesus Christ.”

1 Thessalonians 1:3

DEVOTION

Cause and effect are happening in this verse. Faith produces work, love prompts serving, and hope in Jesus gives strength to endure. It was the same for Jesus. He was able to endure the cross because He knew it was the only way to save people like us, and that brought Him joy (Hebrews 12:2). Our ability to keep our eyes on Jesus and continue to put our trust in Him will determine our ability to endure. What's driving you? Is it just the good feelings in the moment? If so, then that can also stop you. God's Word consistently calls us to set, place, and fix our eyes on Him. We need to focus on the hope that transcends the current moments.

QUESTIONS

What work do you feel that faith and love are prompting you to do right now? How is hope giving you the endurance to keep going and not stop?

CONFESSION

I will walk in the faith, hope, and love of God!

"Brothers and sisters, we do not want you to be uninformed about those who sleep in death, so that you do not grieve like the rest of mankind, who have no hope."

1 Thessalonians 4:13

DEVOTION

Losing loved ones is difficult. Depending on how close we were to the individual, it may be more difficult, but regardless, loss requires times of grieving. Because of God's promise of salvation and resurrection for those who are believers in Jesus, we do not have to mourn like those who have no hope. Because we are fully human, we're going to experience all of the human emotions, but because of Jesus, we don't have to drown in those emotions. We can grieve with peace. How? When you experience loss of life, look to Jesus.

QUESTIONS

Share about a time when you lost a loved one. How was your grieving process? What helped you find hope again?

CONFESSION

I will have hope even in death. I will see in heaven all those who follow Christ on earth!

45

“But since we belong to the day, let us be sober, putting on faith and love as a breastplate, and the hope of salvation as a helmet.”

1 Thessalonians 5:8

DEVOTION

Hope is a helmet. Hope is an insulation against the mental attack of the enemy. One of the main ways that the enemy attacks us is through our minds—getting us to think in a way that is destructive to our lives and future. But, just like a helmet protects your physical head from injury, hope in Jesus protects your mind from the attack of the enemy. This is why the devil is always going to try to steal your hope and leave you unprotected. If the enemy can get us thinking hopeless thoughts, he'll start getting you to live that way. Like the Bible says, take every thought captive (2 Corinthians 10:5)!

QUESTIONS

Why does the Bible describe faith and hope as armor? How can you remain in hope despite all of the bad news?

CONFESSION

God will guard my heart and mind as I put my hope in Him!

46

"Command those who are rich in this present world not to be arrogant nor to put their hope in wealth, which is so uncertain, but to put their hope in God, who richly provides us with everything for our enjoyment."

1 Timothy 6:17

DEVOTION

We should work hard and create wealth like the Bible tells us we've been given the power to do. But where is your hope and trust? Is it in the economy? Is it in the latest stock market strength? Is it in the housing market? Or is your hope in Jesus? The truth is that even if you make all the right moves financially, there's going to be difficult seasons and an economy you can't control. Should that make you afraid? No, because your stability isn't found in those factors but in the reliability of God's economy. God can give you a strategy to be blessed even in famine.

QUESTIONS

Have you experienced sudden loss? How did you recover? How can you make sure you have money rather than money having you?

CONFESSION

I will not put my hope in money. I will trust in God.

47

"God did this so that, by two unchangeable things in which it is impossible for God to lie, we who have fled to take hold of the hope set before us may be greatly encouraged. We have this hope as an anchor for the soul, firm and secure. It enters the inner sanctuary behind the curtain, where our forerunner, Jesus, has entered on our behalf. He has become a high priest forever, in the order of Melchizedek."

Hebrews 6:18-20

DEVOTION

Hope is an anchor! An anchor grounds us, stabilizes us, and keeps us from being tossed back and forth by the wind and the waves. We can be tossed by things above and below the surface, but the anchor holds us securely. Today, get your life anchored in Christ. How? By getting connected to the church community. In the house of God, you get around like-minded followers of Christ who are letting down their anchor into Christ. In the world, we're getting told not to put too much hope or trust in the Bible, but this lack of certainty is creating pain and confusion. Choose to drop the anchor of trust into Jesus and His Word today.

QUESTIONS

What's a lie that the culture is trying to force you to accept?
How has trusting Jesus changed your life?

CONFESSION

I am secure because my hope is anchored in Jesus!

48

"Let us hold unswervingly to the hope we profess, for he who promised is faithful."

Hebrews 10:23

DEVOTION

Let's focus on the profession of your hope! Are you speaking and declaring hope? What are you actually saying out loud? What are you consistently confessing and professing over your life? That's why we wrote a confession for each devotional to get your confessions infused with hope. You may need to write the promises of God on your mirror or post them around your home—whatever you need to do to be sure you hold unswervingly to the hope of Jesus. Biblical confession transforms your heart and mind, which then transforms your life!

QUESTIONS

Would your friends say that you are a hopeful person? Are you confessing hope or fear? Write down three hope-filled statements about your future and read them out loud until you believe them!

CONFESSION

I will declare the promises of God over my life!

49

“Now faith is confidence in what we hope for and assurance about what we do not see.”

Hebrews 11:1

DEVOTION

Hope is the vehicle that faith rides in on. Hope is the atmosphere for faith, and faith brings heaven to earth. What are you hoping for right now? What are you stretching for in faith? God wants you to trust Him for the dream, calling, and promises that are beyond your reach. The promises that God gave to Abraham, to build a nation from his offspring when he had no children, were so far beyond him. When Abraham would get off track because of doubt and delays, God would call him back to remember His promises. Those God encounter moments would renew his hope and cause him to trust God again!

QUESTIONS

What are you believing God for that you don't see yet? What role does hope play in your faith?

CONFESSION

Hope is the foundation of faith, and Jesus is the reason for my hope.

50

“Praise be to the God and Father of our Lord Jesus Christ! In his great mercy he has given us new birth into a living hope through the resurrection of Jesus Christ from the dead.”

1 Peter 1:3

DEVOTION

Often when people talk about church, they think of religion and rules, but God calls us into a living and alive relationship with Him. Your salvation isn't into a dead religion but a living hope. Have you ever been looking at an owner's manual and realized it's for an older model of vehicle? That manual isn't going to be able to help you because it's outdated. But when God gave us His Word in written form, these are not dusty history lessons that are outdated; they are fresh and living and relevant for our lives today.

QUESTIONS

What has God been doing in your heart as you've studied through these verses on hope? What has God brought back to life in you that felt hopeless?

CONFESSION

My hope is alive in Jesus! I do not fear because He is with me!

51

"Therefore, with minds that are alert and fully sober, set your hope on the grace to be brought to you when Jesus Christ is revealed at his coming."

1 Peter 1:13

DEVOTION

Did you know you have a hope bank? And you have a choice where to set and invest that hope. Set your hope on God's grace. His grace is so powerful because His grace isn't dependent on my performance or what I say; it's based on Him. The stock market rises and falls based on issues of the day. But God continues to show us kindness no matter our issues and challenges. And it's on this unearned grace that we put our hope. So, my hope is sure and strong because I don't have to worry if God will be different next week or next year than He is today.

QUESTIONS

How have you learned to receive the grace of God in the middle of your failures? How are you daily choosing hope?

CONFESSION

God's grace allows me to continue in hope even when I fail.

52

"But even if you should suffer for what is right, you are blessed. 'Do not fear their threats; do not be frightened.' But in your hearts revere Christ as Lord. Always be prepared to give an answer to everyone who asks you to give the reason for the hope that you have. But do this with gentleness and respect, keeping a clear conscience, so that those who speak maliciously against your good behavior in Christ may be ashamed of their slander."

1 Peter 3:14-16

DEVOTION

We'll wrap up these fifty-two verses on hope by calling all of us to continue to spread love and hope to the world around us. You have encountered the hope that is in Jesus. Now, are you ready to give a reason for that hope? Why are you hopeful? Why are you full of joy? Why did you give your life to that hope? When you're sharing your hope, begin with just sharing your story about how Jesus changed your life. You don't have to have all the right words; just share your personal experience with Christ. When you share that story, you'll invite others into the journey, and they will want the hope that you have. Or the Hope that has you!

QUESTIONS

Do you feel comfortable talking about God with your friends? Who are three people that you can share with about your hope in Jesus and invite to church? Commit to pray for them and share boldly with them.

CONFESSION

I will be ready to give the reason for this great hope!

ABOUT THE AUTHOR

Samuel is a passionate follower of Jesus, in love with his beautiful wife, Katie, and loves being a father to his two incredible girls, Mercedes and Kenzie. He and his wife are a part of the pastoral team at Awaken Church in San Diego, California. They also serve the broader Church community through a discipleship resource called "Following Jesus" and by preaching and ministering with a prophetic edge!